The Devil's Egg

Steven Joseph
McCrystal

ISBN: 9798333811349

All Rights Reserved
Steven Joseph McCrystal ©2024

Art work front cover Steven Joseph McCrystal ©2024
Front Cover "*The Devil's Egg*"

Steven has asserted his moral rights

Inherit The Earth
©2024

Published by Inherit The Earth in conjunction with
Amazon KDP ©2024

Edited by CT Meek

First published 2024

The Devil's Egg -
This is Steven's latest poetry offering. It follows on from Stabilizer, The Wrong Messiah, Nuts And Thunderbolts, Exotic Species, Monkey Spit, and Red Pill Memories. He's an industrious and creative soul who best expresses himself in his writing and unique artistic style (he created this book cover). He continues to struggle with his own demons, and writes openly from a personal perspective about mental health issues. His candour is something to be admired. Hopefully it can help others.

Meek
Editor/Publisher
July 2024

Contents
A Feather's Caress
A Good Place
A Heart's Desire
Anti-Woke Joke
Big Hopes, Distant Dreams
Bright Eyes
Complex Creatures
Cthulhu Speaks
Dark Roads, Bright Lights
Elemental Seductress
Flowers For The Girls
Give Me Glimmers
Glory Spots
God's Holey Trousers
Grass Is Greener
Halfway There
He Was Saw The Deep
Hello Red Pill
I Hope I See Rainbows
Justice Tree
Love Struck Sonnet
Manufactured Bliss
Mission Status Go
Monkey's Paw
Moonbeam And Dreams
Needful Things
Nemesis
One Year Older
Pinball Wizard

Requiem Of A Dream
Shame The Braineater
Something Beautiful
Starry, Starry Night
Strange Universe
The Chase Hurdles
The Dream
The Kiss
The Nature Of Things
The Red Mist
To The Moon And Back
Underneath The Oak
Valentines
Wake Up Neo
We Want Togetherness
When The Storm Comes It Comes
When Will Love?
World On Fire
Writer's Revenge
Yesterday
You Bring Light In

A Feather's Caress
Stop, it tickles, your feathers caress
Enticing me to perform and digress
Into a loving and emotive wilderness
Leave pains behind like it was nothingness

Show love, real energy, to humanity
Rise, ascend from your love calamities
Tickle yourself and become a fan of me
A guide for your confusing insanities

My feathers caress can make your heartbeat faster
Make you withstand any emotional disaster
Repair your heart with a band aid plaster
And show you love my one true master

My feathers can show you smiles from a passer by
Coy looks from a beautiful fluttering butterfly
That make you ponder and wonder why
My karmic good fortune will make you sigh

I'll be a friend for life once you pick me up
Tune in and raise me like the proverbial pup
I'll be your angel so let's sit down and sup
Chew the fat and ask what the fucks up?

The only question: will you be a friend of me?
I need this sublime level of age old clarity
So, we can both achieve a level of serenity
To form ticklish feathers for my new identity

A Good Place
Where would we be without a good place to see
Where everything in your mind is absolutely ace and free
Mines is unrequited past loves. That ultimate Nirvana
Where memories of love hint at the proverbial bananas
It grows my garden of hope and exquisite mind flowers
My damaged heart still walks through the fragrant bowers
Memories of good times, good feelings, and good connections
And the hope the new love is a cure with a soulful correction
In my mind it's love that's going to rekindle the inferno
Get my heart pumping like a horse towards the next furlough
Everybody needs a good place to be during the bad days
Whether it be subliminal plays in the summer haze
Friends and family making their crucial indelible mark
Or self-love: streaking naked would be a good place to start

A Heart's Desire

A heart's desire is another heart
Someone to hold when the loving starts
Someone to capture all of your giggles
Someone to love all your little niggles
Someone who whistles when your bum wiggles
A heart that wants to dance the night away
Getting closer and closer each and every day
Soaring blindly on the cusp of a tidal wave
Good vibrations are all the things that you gave
Emotions connected like birdsong in the morn
A prince or princess for your gifts to adorn
Sweet music flutters the heart of the lost and found
A companion heart, best friends, is beyond sight or sound
Often the cause of feet not touching the ground

Anti-Woke Joke
Can you love everyone all of the time?
Be peaceable, dig deep, believe that everybody is kind
Change the world like the hippies did in 1969
People are standing up to this idea of woke
We are unique, not the same, and that's no joke
I've never been part of the group collective
Whilst making friends I've always been selective
I'm not trying to be nasty but it's becoming a joke
I'm not trying to be bad, but a bloke is a bloke
If I dressed up as a lion and identified as a cat
Would you believe me if you examine my cat stats?
Love tells us to give in to an unachievable equality
That we are loved by each and every piece of humanity
No derision, no difference, no precision this time
No character building from our struggles and grime
I want to be different, stand out, not be the same
Find my unique love in humanities crying game
Where do we begin? Where and when did it all start?
When did we start blubbering about mother nature's hearts
What would Walt Disney say if he was alive and awake?
Would he scream woke until he found out it was fake?
Is this just a Western life philosophy that's being made?
Love should not leave you feeling ever so slightly afraid
That your uniqueness is swirling deeper down the drain
That love is a battle being fought with absolutely no refrain
Thirty years from now we'll call it the equality wars
A steam roller trundling over our hopes and fears
More people stripped of their individuality for years and years

There's a huge difference between being accepted and being an equal
Is there room for another bad ass and natural deep thinking sequel
We're not even born the same because of the X and the Y
Thankfully, I will remain an X and a Y until the day that I die
I'm old school though, 54, I was brought up in a different era
So now I'm too old tackle this roaring and glaring Chimera
But we can't say anything now it's way too late
All we can do is leave our mixed-up hearts to fate

Big Hope, Distant Dreams
I've had hope dangled in front of me like the Donkey's carrot
An antidepressant for up in the attic
The final ascent up the mountain to the land of hopes and dreams
Has begun in earnest. A calling for butterfly wings and dreams
The last clamber. It has to be. Just reach out it and grab it seems
23 long years, a soul that's been bombed and scrambled,
so intense, a crucible of dreams not managed, a life which has to be worked at
A second mind persistently nagging, nudging, goading like a parrot
An ageless observer chiding with the incessant voice of a youth
Get on it. Do it. Follow the plan. There will be no excuse
My own personal Nirvana awaits and there's nothing to lose
May I rest in peace when I find it this ill-fated muse?
More work to reach the realms of Xanadu
More work to tame the crazy life at the zoo
More work that will be a twisted pleasure to do
Retirement plans forming under foot
Just one last clamber has taken root

Bright Eyes
I see visions of the future all of the time
Grandiose destinations play tricks on my mind
Possibilities that may or may not come true
Something to work towards when I'm not feeling blue
Inspiration none the less even if it's a little askew
But these visions give a distorted utopian view
Where all mythological religions get a reality check
I mean religion, myth, faith, what the feck!
Causes more death than cancer I bet
Collateral damage it has to be ignored a century once said
My damage, a deep cut or two, has got my soul seeing red
A fire inside that's inspiring me to burn, burn, burn
Benevolence, was just around the corner I'm beginning to learn
My before attitude to life lost for decades during the angry strife
Chilled out, matured, for the most part I've lived a philosophical life
But the trouble with yin and yang is the continual fight
To find meaning in the troubles that have plagued your might
My life's purpose to create, compose, and share my wisdom
A positive to be said, but will humanity listen

Complex Creatures
We are all built the same you and I
Brain, heart, lungs, blood, stomach, and teeth
A blank page to be filled out upon our birth
Our emotions are the scriptwriters of our destiny first
This tastes good. This feels bad
This tastes bad. This feels good
Ewww, but I don't want to feel that way
Is that understood?
That's why I'm crying this way
I'll spit the dummy you absolute cad
But I love it in every single way today
Our feelings are not just a fad
Our emotions must be the origin of our soul
Growing, evolving, learning, memorizing
Feeling our wibbly-wobbly way safely home
Making us feel like we belong
Pushing us forward when our gut tells us it's wrong
Fear and love or pleasure and pain
Widening our horizons once again
Love emotions taming the feral beast
Anger protecting tomorrow's feast
What if we were only emotions?
Surely anger would dominate every day
No room for restraint or logic first
Just monsters from the Id beating fast
Experience quenching or incessant thirst
Taste, touch, sight, sound, and smell
Common traits all attached to our emotional soul

Senses setting our hearts and minds on fire
Adding pages and pages of script to the pyre
What a circus of feelings defines us
Primed and ready like a blunderbuss
We can't keep them in because they'll poison us
Good or bad they have to come out
An absolute folly or with an absolute clout
We're all such complex creatures
Survival of the fittest is one of our features
How we survived I'll never know
Protecting our emotions in a community in order to grow
Feeling togetherness, the very essence of our wayward souls

Cthulhu Speaks

I ascend from the depths of a haunted mind
I am the demigod of your nightmares and madness
black swivelling black on dinosaur wing and sadness
My probing eyes wander to those things that are mine.
Your terror belongs to me.
Your fear belongs to me.
Your mind belongs to me.
Your forsaken soul belongs to me
I am possession
I see my things caress my blood ridden eyes just before I bite
With my squid like maw sucking blood in the middle of the night
We are connected you and I
Joined in cascading telepathic psychosis
I see you
Trapped in an ever-descending hypnosis
I see you frozen to the spot
Resisting the Call of Cthulhu's gut twisting knots

Dark Roads, Bright Lights

We often get stuck travelling a road less travelled
You know the one where sleeping beauty doesn't awake
The thorns keep growing as the castle is engulfed by fate
The hero doesn't show up to save the day in their very own way
Hope, your only friend, deserted their companion in the end
Spooks and spirits dominate every bend in the road ahead
Wild eyes scan you from the insidious shadows in the trees
Hyena's and vultures stalk you because you're dead meat walking
The law of the jungle has taken a chunk out of your ass
Things can only get worse no matter what move you make
And a step in the right direction can be the most painful one to make
It may seem like darkness falls with every step you take
But don't be afraid of holding on and travelling into the light
Kick, claw, scream, dig your heels in, by all means fight this shite
Hope, your friend, will return like a flickering glimmer of light
The return of a long-lost friend because you stood up to fight
The road less travelled will straighten up and be less scary
Every inch, every step, every breath taken will be strength you fairy
Eventually endurance will pave the way to an evolution of character
You'll be a veteran, a fighter, a bad ass, an immense soul survivor

After the storm subsides raindrops will be a mere trickle of shite
And the hard road less travelled will be a journey into the light

Elemental Seductress

She is destiny captured on an artist's easel
She plays a fanfare for the common people
You, me and everyone else she happens to see
Warning hearts and minds with merriment and glee
She is of the earth with eyes like emerald mines
Drawing you in deeper to see what you can find
Her heart burns like fire. An element to warm the soul
Her love continuous as her sensual movements flow
Her veracious hunger is for your enthralled appetites
Succumb and become one of my, in orbit satellites
Her loving words, quite simply the air that she breathes
Carry you on a inward journey. They are an illicit tease
A perfect siren of sorts waiting at the water's edge
Waiting patiently and longing for your eternal pledge
Singing songs with smiles like a heavenly angel
Waiting for a deeper love to ignite the inferno

Flowers For The Girl

Why not give your crush a red, red rose
Share some feelings and see how it goes
Make your words complimentary and feminine
Make them serenade like the scent of Jasmine
Raise her heart up to the status of goddess
Give her an exotic orchid to match her finesse
But alas there is no beauty to compare to thee
No flowers or words in the dictionary that I can see
Lovely, delicious, delectable, desirable or divine
Intelligent, smart, canny, brilliant, intuitive or fine
Your heart knows what flowers to bring in this dream
Wild bluebells and snowdrops for your queen
A walk in the wilderness amongst the golden rays
May your love last forever until the end of days

Give Me Glimmers

What is a simple glimmer?
I've never heard of them for a very long while
All my days in fact even when they make you smile
Someone's defined them on one of my therapeutic sites
I thought I'd promote because they're out of sight
Something new with a little bit of soothing style
Soothing hope. Soothing smiles. Soothing all the time
A little happy tickle up and down your spine
A gooey emotion running a little bit wild
Yes, I want this it makes me feel fine
They're the opposite of a trigger so just give me a glimmer
And a little bit of healing will be yours and mine
A small piece of positivity shared between buddies and chums
An encouragement, a compliment, a kindness my friend
An interest in you and what you do pays dividends
So, thanks for all the times you've glimmered me my friend
My heart and soul has turned into a disco full of lights
Instead of the moody grunge party full of goths moshing at night

Glory Spot

Nope, there's no avoiding it
This grandiose destination in my mind
The remnants of altered states of perceptions I find
Trauma the seed for the lighthouse flashing duty in my mind
Playing havoc with my criss-crossed thoughts so kind
No one can see it this compulsion of mine
Just the urge to succeed at the finish line
It's like a cloud of thought hanging like a chandelier
From the roof of my mind and it's encompassed with tears
Burning brightly enough to obscure the view
Burning brightly enough to hypnotise stew
My mind blended by the carnage it's seen
Inspired by ongoing manic and psychotic dreams
But the light compels me to change the world
Produce love if I can through my creative endeavours
Art, poetry, books and lots and, lots of slavers
I suppose the light has to be taken on faith
My guide, my hunger, my compulsions are all a rock solid wraith
Just got to put the work in to my master plan forthwith
Follow the glory spot my mind has created
The world's your oyster sounds so enticing
The light, like a siren, sings its song blindly

God's Holey Trousers

Chosen you have an obligation my friend
To walk the earth on a mission to the end
and stop yourself from going around the bend
Muster up some love and send, send, send
It doesn't matter how brutal your ascension was
Good souls heal and recover to find a purpose in life
Good souls heal. No matter how long. That's life
Married to the moment God kissed you like a lover
Head anointed by your soon to be lifelong brother
You've really got to feel it to believe it
Experience that mind blowing shit
An ocean of God engulfing your puny mind
The vastness of that loving omnipotent feeling so kind
It doesn't matter if you believe or not
The cerebral experience means and says a lot
The memory keeps you company throughout the years
It defies logic and whispers fate in your ears
Drives you in life and gives you wheels to steer
Plies you with hope and endurance to ally your fears
Once kissed theirs is no wall you can't run through
Survive the worst that life has to throw at you
All because an indelible friend possessed your mind
Gave you a quest in life that only you can find
To walk the earth on a mission to the end
Muster up some love and send, send, send

Grass Is Greener

Many of us have dreams of a different life
The one where there has been no trouble and strife
My lawn with flowers is to have some kids and a loving wife
And maintain a job that you love for the rest of your life
I'd go to university and plan for an illustrious career
Have friends that I loved and held really, really dear
I'd love my mum and dad to be alive, healthy and live quite near
So, my kids could visit my parents every week of the year
We'd have parties and barbecues with family and friends
In my beautiful semi-detached house. The one at the end
You'd be invited to my little piece of paradise my friend
I'd send the invites. I mean really send, send, send
Holidays twice a year to Timbuktu as long as we flew
Everything all at once. As long as we all grew and grew
The ideal dream life of perfect perfection but who only knew?
Life would hit you like a ton of heavy bricks that knocks you askew
Bad choices my friend led to this reflective dream of dreams
I hope you choose wisely and don't end up looking like Edvard Munch's Scream
Instead of giving gifts of love like flowers, diamonds, or pearls to your queen

Halfway There

Some journeys take forever to achieve
Many stop halfway there and choose to leave
Gruesome thoughts invade your space
Doubt or pleasure interrupt the race
Your footfalls and mind say I give up
But your heart of hearts just says what's up
I've got to do this epic chore until it becomes a bore
Until the importance of success leaves you sore
Keep going, you must, until we all turn to dust
On top of the mountain, you'll wonder why the fuss
Plod on, make your path, put one foot in front of another
Make determination, perseverance, and willpower your brothers
Get back up when you slip and fall off the edge
Theirs is always something to hold onto, another ledge
May your grip become stronger with each endeavour
May your heart grab the here and now, may it last forever
When you reach your goals may you achieve heart felt bliss
Spin round, dance and twist, as if you've had a juicy almighty kiss

He Who Saw The Deep

Trouble can be found when you are submerged by God
Floating in an omnipotent ocean as vast as love
Intelligent feedback when the connection is made
Insane epiphanies that would make you scream no way
Impossible instructions announced to a befuddled gaze
Do my bidding. Champion my needs. Plant some seeds
A poke in the third eye of the internal maze
A soul coated and cooked in omnipotent honey glaze
A lifelong experience created out of pain and an ocean of love
A subconscious quest ticking away like a doomsday dove
Unravelling its way through time it will never stop
Layer upon layer of insights arise from deep in the depths
Wisdom granted as time tries to heal all wounds it's said
To meet God you need to go through hell
He, she, or it is at the end of an arduous journey into self
Sir Percival, the knight, almost died just for a glimpse of God's love
Was it all in his head? Quite likely. God's internal devices quite frankly
Mother nature's internal devices to put it blankly
I never believed in divinity until it happened to me
As I unravel as all suppressed creatures do.
Only I can see the transformation God has given me
Only I can see the transformation experience has given me
Over time I've had to stew towards acceptance
Quietly, reluctantly, sneakily, messily, secretly
All it cost me was my sanity and soul
But at what cost art?
At what cost poetry?

At what cost prose?
But at what cost wisdom and philosophy?
At what cost the hard eared gifts of the experienced soul
The world will never be the same. Never. I know
One where the source of all religion is grandiose
Created from the mind's imaginations my friend
But I have divine hope now, an angel in my heart
Guiding me to greatness, The compulsion to succeed is limitless
A driving force for the sometimes spiritless
Good deed by good deed is the only way to play
Keep the angels happy so they can guide the way
And I'm playing the slow and steady game
All religious compulsions lead to the public domain
Got to speak. Got to say. It's the only way to make my day
And change my mind in another way

Hello Red Pill
You have a choice, and the choice is the metaphor pill
Flame red, its ingestion: a brutal madness designed to test your will
Sky blue, its ingestion: welcome back to the duvet of tranquillity
What would you choose? A boring lifetime of passive serenity
Or an adventure of insanity for which there is an unknown bill
Evolve, grow, disconnect, break, smash your fragile little mind
You are fucked anyway as soon as you become bipolar ill
Become a freak, run like the wind, be an anomaly for all mankind
Should you gamble your life away in the hope of a better day?
Have dreams of glory that it's you who will save the world one day
Some adventurers have to survive. It's the rules of the game
So, choose the red pill if you still have some wayward youth
Go wild, go reckless, go headless, go totally beyond insane
Come down, recover, recuperate, curl up in a therapeutic ball
Suck you thumbs because you're in a descending free fall
Only one is invited to stare at the reflective disco ball
Reminisce your past looking for answers like an amateur sleuth
Find out that there isn't any kind of contorted existential truth
So, embrace the contract with the devil and inscribe your name
There's one undeniable certainty: you'll never be the same
You might get extremely lucky and out fiddle the little red devil
Stretch, reach out for the stars and end up on a different level

But the right choice is a truly dangerous game.
Take the blue pill and stay the same

I Hope I See Rainbows

I hope I see wish granting rainbows on my way home
Mother nature playing with physics, so we don't feel alone
In the sky and traversing the ground
So that the pots of gold can never be found
If rainbows could sing, they'd make lots of sound
Divine beauty, mother nature's heart completely unwound
Smiles, and fingers pointing up towards the wish
Multi coloured colours with a two tailed swish
Love in your heart as you succumb to the journey
A sunshine flower for my mind called Earnie
We should name our rainbows ever so much
But don't let the guys start because they'll give it a woman's touch
Elanor, Stephanie. Karen, Loo-ka, Cleopatra are all fine names
Peter, Paul, David, Steven. Hamish could be classed as the same
At the finish of your journey, you could do something romantic
Hello, my love, I passed a rainbow today and gave it your name
I can't help it my love It feels like I'm rainbow insane

Justice Tree
Climb this tree at your passionate peril
One branch, one knot, one foot, one claw
Ascending upwards like a disjointed bear
Reaching skywards with each snap of the twig
The promise of justice honey just out on a limb
Just out of reach at every step of the way
Overreached you're destined to fall
Breaking old bones that have nearly healed
Through dint of effort and clambering
Upwards and onwards to the honey pot
A taste of sweetness that would cure all wrongs
Forgive and forget maybe not
Respite from being a bear growling all day long
One more step. One more twig. One more snap
One more hope. One more fall. One more growl
One more ascension from the bottom to the top
Until you've ripped out every branch without stop
Snapped every wayward twig on the way to the top
Clawed at every single nook and cranny
To find the bees nest empty of honey
Not even a ghost of a bee defending its realm
Nothing but emptiness on this solo mission
Even if victory was the final successful destination
Not any sweet honey healing to show for the effort
But it's better to do and fail than not to have tried
On your quest for justice up the justice tree to meet the bees

Love Struck Sonnet

Is it just your damn luck if you find a soul mate?
Or does life conspire against you because of fate?
Each of us is looking for that love struck connection
An electric moment in time that is beyond reflection
Dumb struck hearts beating a blinding thumping tune
Turning their owners into a wanton rapacious loon
Who doesn't want more love, more kisses, more hugs?
When baby Cupid's lightning bolt strikes from above
We can't stop that giddy feeling of love struck love
Nothing like a passionate heart to give your life a shove
Everybody should have at least one loving muse in their lifetime
Everything else is nothing but love's wicked soul crime
Years and years of deep loving your best ever friend
Don't worry, at a loss, I'm sure love will win in the end

Manufactured Bliss

If you drop from the tree like Newton's apple did
Succumb to the gravity of the unreality of life
And end up with a few monsters from the id
If howling at the moon is the only way through the strife
There's a manufactured bliss that is plied into weary souls
Antidepressants, Lithium, Mirtazapine, Risperidone
To get you back to buying manufactured goals
You will never feel the same, human, on permanent postpone
Love conquers all if you're lucky enough to feel it
But not if you're on an emotional manufactured dose
Stealing happiness from the shelves of the supermarket
This makes me happy. That makes me happy. It's not even close
So, we sit in our houses glued to the set like battery hens
Making lifestyle choices only to find more lifestyle choices on another channel
Cock teasing our souls with lifestyle choice dividends
Less damage could be caused by whipping your arse with a hot wet flannel
So, let's give three cheers for this manufactured bliss
You've got to fight through it, break from the norm, fight for your right to exist
Of course, there's a tablet for that if you get carried away
If you find yourself in open fields of follies and flowers some day

Mission Status Go

It's impossible to imagine where I've been
It's impossible to imagine what I've seen
Journeys of the mind stuck in a haunting dream
Journeys of the mind that would make you scream
No amount of therapy can change the trauma
No amount of therapy can switch the heat off in the sauna
But now that I'm older mellowed and mature
I've shovelled all the shit and spread all the manure
My garden grows philosophical flowers and half decent food
To be consumed and shared in my neighbourhood
But fuelling this mission is a God mission a go-go
An experience of mine which I denied and said no to
A delusion of mine that would shake the foundations of any soul
Knuckle down, get on with the job, my son Jesus is a sod
A commandment for me a commandment from God
Remove Jesus from me or face eternal damnation
How, where, why, what is my eternal frustration
What a mind-altering head fuck of a bloody conundrum
Got to do what the big chief says and rid the world of this Beelzebub bum
The answer is a write a book, research, a compulsion of course
More flowers, more manure, a little research of the source
I found the solution that satisfies my compulsion to complete the mission
Hopefully my revelations will go off like nuclear fission
Nearly there, nearly where? My radar is targeting ground zero
I hope my love nuke detonates and makes me an anti-hero

To all those people who have suffered from mental illness because of Jesus
I mean, how long is the church going bend, break, and squeeze us

Monkey's Paw
Monkey's paw, monkey's paw
Would you make a wish for more?
If it came a knock, knock, knocking on your door
Sell your heart and soul to this Indian mutant claw
Live your life with the unknown repercussion
One wish is all it takes change your luck into a deception
Heart slipping and sliding to its final macabre destination
Cursed wishes of the innocent corrupted so
W.W. Jacobs asking if you want some pain to go
Curled fingers one by one gripping your heart
Fearfully praying until the final wish is done

Moonbeams And Daydreams

Do all dreams shine like moonbeams?
A little touch a lunacy from the night
A wish made from within your dreams
A wish made when travelling into the light
Sunshine or rainbows or wishing upon a star
Have no permanence but lunacy will take you far
Night after night and day after day
The moon will shine in its indelible way
Possessing your mind with promises from the deep
Enticing actions only your intoxicated body can keep
Possessed by a dream in the waking hours
Lunacy might become your lover and bring you flowers
The more you dance in amongst the moonbeam bowers
The more you dance in amongst the storms and showers

Needful Things

Human beings are such needful things
We need bits and bobs of everything
A little bit of love to send us on our way
A little bit of love to make us stay
Our emotions can be our latest craze
Or keep us distant and out of phase
Wholeheartedly addicted to a lover's call
Braving the tempests of a lover's squall
To find peace and love in their embrace
Winning Darwin's evolutionary race
I am at a loss myself, a needful thing
A bird of paradise that cannot sing
My heart has been chopped and churned
Set on fire and burned and spurned

Nemesis
Have you ever been inclined to defeat an indomitable soul?
You dig deep to do battle, practice, find out their flaws and go
Repeatedly head-butting a rock would cause less of a fuss
A flurry of fists in your mind appears after each and every cuss
In round one you had no hope at all. You get totally mauled
Lost at sea in the storms. Engulfed by the waves and the rising squall
In round two, you are partially prepared but still the onslaught is sore
You take another beating but this time you study the creature some more
In round three, you've learned, recovered, adapted, acquired some skill
But you wait patiently, tirelessly, without moving in for the inevitable kill
The creature grows in your mind bigger than any hot air balloon
Your friends tell you, express their woes, oh my god you are a loon
Years of study, work, shadow boxing in your troubled mind
Can only lead to the big event, mano on mano, could this round be kind
Will the punters listen, watch, or even defend our illustrious champ
One knockout blow, cut the Achilles heel, something I've studied at base camp

All it will take, and this is for real, is an uppercut of truth amongst the unreal
Thanks, my nemesis for all that you've done. Thanks for giving me all of that zeal

One Year Older

Cheers, another new year passes by with a bang
Raise your glasses in a celebratory toast
Time for your new year's resolution boast
We survived another year and our hearts sang
Another year older and wiser my friend
Could this be the year that pays dividends?
Another year of lost causes on the mend
Boyfriend girlfriend kisses at the stroke of the bells
Sister, brother, husband and wife asking if all is well
Hugs and kisses underneath the shadow of the mistletoe
But, where the fuck does all the time go
Hands clasped together for auld lang syne
Because tonight you are a friend of mine
Happy New Year and may your fortunes be fine
Have a prosperous and fabulous new year this time
Day one it's tradition to feel like a burst ball gone south
It was fun at the time when opening your mouth
Shake my hand. I'm wishing you a happy new year
Get the champagne, make mine a wine, let's say cheers with a beer
This year's going to be just fine

Pinball Wizard

The flipper flips for another go
Trying to save your balls from going down a hole
Trying to avoid the emotional tilt
Frustration consumes and is always felt
Psychiatrists, psychologists, nurses, I play the game
I have many points scored with the stainless steel ball
Going up and down and around and around again
Hoping, just hoping, to rise up and not fall
Flat on my face where I am just now
Stifled and stagnant and unable to glow
Apart from bitch, bitch, bitch
Moan, moan, moan
Waiting for the plunger to be pulled again
By hope that I get a good run and a high score
That happiness picks me up off the floor
A bipolar life is a tough game to master
Happy meds restricted in case of disaster
But I'll have another go on the pinball machine
Because I have many bipolar dreams

Requiem For A Dream

An obsessional dream is a compulsion of sorts
It consumes your life and consumes your thoughts
On a good day it gives you visions to reach out and hope
On a bad day it gives you frustrations that aren't very dope
But good or bad. Success or failure. It gives life substance
A chance for your hearts to sing and dance
A complex desire to win and nail her
Don't let go, don't give up, travel the road even if it's coloured yellow
And flying monkeys scream and swoop and yell at you
One of those footsteps will undoubtedly land on a mellow
A compulsion appeased by a little bit of success I tell you
And hope your machine mind is greased for the next
The next step of the yellow brick road which is seen and seized on a quest
Let the lifelong visionary journey continue
I'm talking years and years of building on your grandiose dreams
Without it there would be no purpose in life so be careful it seems
Without it there would just be an empty head space
There would be no big fat pudding race
Only a mind abandoned on a desert island in the middle of an ocean
But enough about the loneliness and compulsion of desolate dreams
Build a raft out of your last remaining tree of beams

And set sail into the mists of everlasting hope
Let the motion of the waves rescue you from a long distance float
Into your visions and dreams to turn the world on its head
Before your life passes by and you wind up dead
Without your monumental epitaph being seen, heard, or read
Go, go, go my darlings chase the dreams inside your heart and head

Shame The Braineater
Just over the hill and around the corner
Through the mountain and across the ocean
There is a land of freedom and space
Where I can speak about it becomes a place
A place where dark secrets collide and fizzle out
Shame no longer exists and has no power to twist and shout
Confidence returns with a sense of freedom installed
Something stale from the stagnant years leaves you standing tall
And crawls away back into the gutter where it belongs
 A respite break from the same old shame songs
New life, new thoughts, new life at last, just a thought
A wee terrible growling beastie captured and caught
Secrets exposed to friends or in the public domain
The freshness of honesty has been reclaimed
Feeling almost human once again my friend
After decades of shame piled up in the end.
That was driving you round the bend
Non vocal villains, thoughts, in at the deep end
Easier talking to professional folks about your woes
Big pink knickers in a twist as the saying goes
Trust restored. Insanity explored. Shame ignored
Drunk on freedom I'm well and truly floored
Progress attained and all I need is my humour to return
My mind shifting and contorting in an old fashioned gurn
I've been so fucking serious for so many fucking years
Like a drill boring into my mind because of my fears

Lighten up, add some lube, peek right through
All the news is out there to be perused
It's not a cure. Just some simple liberations
With these sense of freedom revelations

Something Beautiful

I wish I had something truly beautiful to say
Something priceless and true and without delay
Make you wish. Make you smile. Make your day
But it's always love that makes you swing and sway
Just one little word in amongst the colour grey
That send heart pumping fireworks into the fray
A drunken head spinning with words like ole ole
A kiss and a cuddle are a prelude to ticklish foreplay
A time in life where hearts and souls come out to play
A seductive bed where we can both love and lay
Open hearts run free at any age in love's sweet cabaret
When two become one. When two becomes they
All we can do is hold our jealous hearts and pray
That maybe, just maybe, it will be us some day

Starry, Starry Night
(Inspired by Graeme Barclay's photograph)

I wonder what the ancients thought slipping into their dreams at night
Staring up at the nocturnal sky cozied in by the campfire light
The pin pricks of dots and suns illuminating our night-time eyes
What is out there? I hear you say way beyond our midnight skies
Did we have children playing and dancing under the midnight suns
Naming patterns and shapes. A constellation of ultimate fun
Draco the dragon whose heart shines on and on like a diamond in the sky
Leo the lion whose roar can be seen, not heard, leaves you wondering why
Gods and beasts decorate our hearts and minds, but we are just small fry
Ascension to the heavens guaranteed when we prepare to die
Will our souls rise up and become the very heart of a star?
Will we travel like the energy of light to distant dreams both near and far?
Will we reach the nearest star so far away but so much out of sight?
In our own personal spaceship that imagined long distance space flight

Different worlds and different places dancing around stars in the making
Will we meet intelligent beings out there because our hearts are breaking?
Light years away and looking back at us with alien kids making all the fuss
Are we part of their constellations? Will we become one? Will we become us?

Strange Universe

I often wonder why we worship forsaken idols
Hope and hearts diminishing in ever decreasing circles
When does gooder than good become badder than bad
A delusion of the mind for innocents and the weary
How does the church escape from its own divine judgement
For all its sins and the women witches burned at the stake, fuck sake
All the wars and the mental illness it has buried to be good
Promoting the lies and non-reality of any divine saviour
Surely, we've grown up now and can find our own guidance
And surely, we can put heaven and hell way behind us
But perhaps we need fantasy and fiction to comfort our souls
Our one time on earth measured and marked by the dying
We need to celebrate our one life during its wonderful passing
Dare I say, celebrate our life, not death, for the saddest of funeral victims
Hope that they appear in our dreams to remind us; one day or night
That they are still here in our hearts wanting to celebrate life with us
Who wants to live forever or forever be eternal married to the dust

The Chase Hurdles

Before you get to the reality of rejection
Be aware there's hurdles in front of your flirtations
Don't be too needy a desperate man dies
Don't be too sensitive a delicate man cries
Don't be too pushy an insistent man starts fires
Don't be too flirty a salacious man fails
Don't be too slow but be patient so love can grow
Don't be too cool she could turn to ice
Don't listen to the advice of your friends
They'll get it wrong again and again
Don't listen to my advice because I'm stuck in limbo
Don't listen to my advice because I'm stuck in limbo
Scared to move in case I blow it. Simple
Once, twice, and thrice around the lover's bend
All arms and legs and head akimbo
Something I'm prone to in the end
Listening to all the does and don'ts my friend
Of my rejection demons guarding my feelings
My heart pumping you just need to be honest
Check the hurdles again you're running through a forest
Keep it simple, be yourself, and once again be honest
That's the best advice I can give but if opportunity knocks
Take your time, you'll grow on her, something you always do
So don't be a klutz and just pull up your socks
And straighten all those hurdles you've already ran through

The Dream

I would recommend to everyone to find an absorbing dream
Start at point A then head to point B and keep on travelling
Don't let doubt or failure stop your heart from unravelling
Carry your passion to the end until your mind is weak and lean

Hard work and effort carry its own reward
Even if success is a fleeting notion
Carry on and embrace every emotion
A heart will strengthen through the humbling discord

Shoot for the stars if you must, pick yourself up from the dust
Keep going until you achieve your dreams
Make it your secret passion in life it seems
Practice and make perfect when you're going boom or bust

There's no such thing as a straight line to success
More like climbing a mountain, a cliff, or glacier at best
May your efforts bring forth wisdom to feather your nest
All this hard core substance is yours to possess

Just keep going until your life comes to an awesome end
Success or failure you've bolstered your heart
All you have to do is find somewhere to start
Maybe one day you'll find fame and fortune my friend

Chasing your dreams to an unknown destination
Navigating by the twinkling stars at night
Chasing rainbows until they're out of sight
Can you feel it? The undiscovered anticipation

The Kiss
Our eyes close travelling towards our tender destination
Seeking electrifying pleasures from this age-old sensation
It truly is one of man and woman's all time fascinations
A twisting wet and moist motion of rhythmic connections
Body all a quiver holding on to feral, illicit trepidations
Roaming paws caressing hearts into wilful submissions
Needful things, chest pumping like a beat with satisfactions
The embrace, head held tight for more intense gratifications
A lover's crushed bodies lost in the realms of lustful attraction
At long last I'll see them in all their glory my love infatuation
Only clothes hide the mind from its sensual imagination
The last barrier between the ongoing, pressing love action
Kissing mouth, kissing neck, kissing shoulders, kissing passion
The tender lips placed lightly is full blown love ammunition
Assume the position!
We're aiming for the ultimate earth shuddering liberation
She: it's time to talk about the inevitable must have protection
He: Oh my God, it's a passion killer this unspoken stipulation
She: In this day and age, we can't afford the ramifications
He: I'm hoping you had the responsible contraception?
He: I'll just pull out before my explicit final destination
He: Too late, my little man has achieved an explosive ejaculation
She: Yes, time for another twenty minutes of kissing and fornication

The Nature Of Things

How many people does it take to change the nature of things?
Brass bands, trumpets, big boss drums, a desire to sing?
An epic commitment in causality consciousness
Does one person jump up and shout this is wrong?
Do those affected congeal together and burst into song?
Should it be suffering that gives the movement that vital spark?
What if the target is perceived as good but in truth is undeniably bad?
For the victims that is
But the goodness trundles along completely unaware of the damage it's done
Churning out more victims that disappear under the melancholy sun
Do we bite the bullet, accept our losses, brush it under the proverbial rug
Hang our victims in the closet or give them a weak voice that tries to tug
At the nature of things
Look what happened to me, I'm scarred to the bone, bruised you see
I've suffered greatly, and there's no justice out there to appease and heal me
Should the victim have to fight just to get their whimpers heard
Fight, fight, fight, I hear you say. Use it or lose it on the battlefield
Do you have the gumption? Do you have the might?
Do you have the wounds that justify your plight?

Fight, set sail on an ocean full of sorrows at each and every turn
Corporate religion can do no wrong. It's for the masses at every turn
You can't sue Jesus or God. Invisible creatures. Invisible torment, Invisible myth no more because I chose to speak
Cries from a desperate soul, a tiny ravaged mind
Just tolerate, endure, carry. Just tolerate, endure, carry, remove joy and delight
Only give a warning to other mental health travellers during the night
Stay away from the cross and the mental sickness that it brings
It's nothing but a double-edged poisonous blade that cuts you in half and pulls you apart
A splinter in your mind that needs Sisyphus work and a calming salve
To oil your own intellect with hope that melancholy will be a brighter place

The Red Mist
It's always the last straw that makes you snap
Your heart broken with all this gas-lighting crap
Shrinks are the worst at not listening to what you have to say
Bang, bang, bang, goes your head of the wall every fuckin day
Whereas before you had the heart of an angel
A persona grown and nurtured from all the good angles
A heart that believes it's wrong to display any kind of anger
Can cause problems, an explosion, when confronted by danger
You feel it, the steam rising, until you lose adrenal control
Fight or flight going into overdrive and scarring your soul
Happiness and pleasantness have been your only goal
But tears of sadness have consumed and taken their toll
Journeys of the mind that only the ferry man knows
As desperation seeps inside your soul and grows and grows
The light, the hope at the end of the tunnel goes out at night
Leaving the human being to gather their strength and might
Stand up tall and continue, continue to fight the nasty gaslight

To The Moon And Back
Buckle up. Grab on. Fasten your seat belts
You are going on the ride of your life, somewhere solo
No one else can go on this no man's land adventure
You'll fight King Kong and Godzilla bare handed
Develop scars and wounds and deep seated trauma
Lose your mind and be branded a fool like you ought ta
Be left with a sense of deep-seated injustice at your failure
Sing songs like; I will survive by Gloria Gaynor
Your soul will pine away to sort out this mess
Because you stood up to a huge, big bastard bully at best
Who couldn't care less
Who couldn't care less
You know what they say about yolo
But everyone on this mission went solo
The trick is to learn how to control the bipolar yoyo
Although the battle was like hell on earth
Three whole years on the slopes of Skull Island
Lost in the jungle of mania and delusion
Pieces of brain scattered about this inhospitable Ghostland
A mind left in tatters like Nagasaki after the bomb
Psychiatric Vietnam fought under the moonlit dome
The worst an adventurer could possibly go through
The worst no choices folly anyone could pursue
But . . .
Logic suggests . . .
Wisdom suggests . . .
Philosophy suggests . . .
Religion suggests . . .

Therapy suggests . . .
Time suggests . . .
I should let things slide into the rubble of my old life
But my trauma memories Nag no, Nag no
So, I'm left with a great big pile of trouble and strife
Reshaping, rebuilding, rewiring is a constant chore
It only takes a bump in the night to give me ghosts galore
But there is hope to be found in amongst the rubble
Ghosts can become friends
Tools in the end
Wounds can become wisdom
Poetry I send
Scars can become sound
I will survive again
And life goes on like a merry go round
You can find the right friends who help you laugh at your tears
There's a cynical and sarcastic sense of humour in your later years
A life less ordinary can become good
I hope that's understood
You may shine like a diamond in amongst the coals
Make your impossible mission one of your life goals
And find nourishment and substance for your very own soul
All of these sacred healing things take time to mature and grow
Good luck with the stability of your lost and wayward soul

Underneath The Oak

300 years to grow
300 years to live
300 years to die
I've sat there underneath the old oak
Wondering what clouds will come out to play
Bathing under the canopy of shade
Sheltered by the gnarled spirit of the old oak tree
Mind dancing with naked nymphs in utter glee
Connected, I hope to the oak's long lived spirituality
Pagan princesses holding hands for a hug
Arms wrapped around and talking profound
I love you tree. I love you tree. I love you tree
Singing and spinning until they hit the ground
Amidst the daisies scattered in circles and floral dots
In between hugs, sun, wind, rain, and snow
Steadfast and strong this acorn has grown slow
Transcending many lifetimes and summer fairs
Embraced by the pagan's springtime prayers
This oak will sing you a lullaby on a hot summer's night
To watch your dreams as you drift and sleep tight
This oak is life eternal, 900 years or more, eternal
Reaching high, reaching broad, reaching tall

Valentines

I look forward to this expression of love
Hearts touched together as if they were one
Love inspired by every single romance created
Love expressed like the colourful wings of a turtle dove
A heart can be found on this day of cupid's arrows
Where that leads is a pumping passion of course
Lips kissed, souls touched, and a smidgeon of lust
Let's hope you arrow doesn't lead to terminal sorrows
Red roses become more beautiful on this day of days
They smell sweet like love is the only elixir of life
Draw drops of blood like no other flower could
But still we ask or valentine to come out to swing and sway
If you're looking but your heart does not find a way
Send a card, a flower, a poem in an anonymous play

Wake Up Neo

I wonder if I'm the biological anomaly in my own little world
Coded, programmed with attitude, I stand alone
I look out, gobsmacked at a planet full of agent Smiths
Shepherding the sheep with their idea of bliss
The TV, media, and internet coercing our emotions
Tackling our anger without any unsightly commotions
Social media, the great placatory tool, soothing our very souls
A platform, a soap box, a band stand for a head full of moans
But what would do without it? How would we achieve our goals?
Advert upon advert upon advert it's just a marketing tool
CEO's making billions from one too many jacked in fools
Am I a hypocrite? I use it all. But I feel that I'm going against the grain
Rebelling, venting, chastising, on an epic mission to use my brain
I'm just one man, unplugged, I've seen the crazy side of humanity
But wish to return, a prodigal son, to the worldwide community
With tales, revelations, and sad and happy stories of my own stupidity
I wish my ending will be on par with a good Hollywood movie
But the matrix isn't real, maybe, or is it already in our mind?
Preprogrammed I feel from all the mixed media you can find
The only way to see, feel it, sense it is through a grandiose delusion
My ultimate insight from a heavy duty 1960's acid trip full of confusion

Wake up Neo, go free range, or stay tuned in a cage like a plucked battery hen
Fake news is about to consume you it's just a case of where and when

We Want Togetherness

If only we could love loads and loads all of the time
Share our feelings without it being a thought crime
Switch our minds on to that lots of love attitude
Put the love of the sixties to shame for once and for good
Have a core concept of community is my platitude
Love's family on your doorstep keeping it right
Love's family on your doorstep keeping it bright
Love's family on your doorstep keeping it real
They say that love will conquer the world we feel
Bring hearts together and inspire it completely
A new level of understanding achieved discreetly
Join hands now because we want togetherness
Begin your journey and travel in from the wilderness
Bring the people who challenge you more or less
Use your life to strengthen, heal, and love them never the less
Join your mind's cogs and wheels to others who feel
Who are driven by love's long and unending zeal
In our minds there is the ability to love more
Will you join us as we stroll through that door
Strip our egos and negative consciousness away
Hold on tight and allow love to conquer the world one day

When The Storm Comes It Comes
I feel the pressure building deep inside my guts
I feel the steam hissing before I'm about to go nuts
So, buckle up Dorothy because Kansas is going bye bye
Elemental forces are about to make you weep and cry
A chemical reaction brewing in my tiny little brain
A little pushy triggered spark is where it begins
Ignition of my tinderbox heart and tinderbox brain
Akin to poking a million bees with a rattling stick
Onlookers only see a raging prick not someone who is sick
It doesn't take much when the red rag is a go go
I force every ounce of self-control out of my soul
I don't want to get mad or angry or view my own wrath
It's literally a poison corrupting and creating an unwelcome warpath
Electrifying my fragile mind, body, and tortured spirit
Contain it, suppress it, swallow it, I just don't want to give it
It's as ugly as sin to any audience members that see it
Someone losing control, exploding, yes, I become a huge big tit
I never used to be like that because I was a peace loving hippie
But sometimes my biochemistry gets a little bit snippy
Because life baptized me with hellfire for three very long years
Going nuclear again has been one of my biggest fears
Good they said, it will clear out the clogged gutters
A constructive outlook from my patient therapist mutters
A little disaster of suppressed elemental proportions
Shifting and grinding away like tectonic forces
A personality corrupted by its ugly distortions
Is there peace? Yes, just don't push any of my buttons
You'll fry my brain like a piece of tenderised mutton

Thankfully, I was blessed with a polite and peaceful outlook
You couldn't tell that I was a wrathful and bitter crook
With a monster of the Id lurking inside my ingle nook
I mean no harm and always choose to walk away
That must be understood, recover and learn to fight my wrath another day
But every few years it rears its mean ugly head
Just when it appears to be well and truly dead
If I had a genie wish or three to make my life better
My suppressed anger would be on the top of the letter

When Will Love

When will love find a way to navigate the hate?
When will love finally give the world a break
When will love leave togetherness in its wake
When will love be left from what we make
When will love invigorate the human race
When will love be the smile upon your face
When will love be the thing that we embrace
When will love become an expression of our grace
When will love cure and wholeheartedly heal the world
When will love become passionate like a rushing rip curl
When will love define us like all love unfurled
When will love be on our side and take our hearts on a burl
When will love seek out and find every nook and cranny
When will love change us so we don't become insanity

World On Fire

Imagine seeing a vision of a burning world
There's no need . . .
We can see it from the comfort of our home
An image left in your mind that has our guts churning
How would you fix this apocalyptic vision?
Without just turning off the television
How would you solve this outright life derision?
Wars, famine, conquest, and death gathering fast
Future revelations from the good book
The anonymous spouter must have been a maniac or a crook
However accurate they were in their visions
Our minds are being blasted to smithereens
There's nothing but war on our media screens
Famine striking Afghanistan, Ethiopia, Haiti, and more
How did we get here? How did we open that door?
Covid infections waiting in the wings, 19, 20, 21
The doomsday countdown begins
World economies on the brink of a virtual collapse
Oh hell, I think I'm on the brink of another relapse
Climate change is fucking relentless
But all our stomachs couldn't care less
Our hearts are being banished from our souls
Slowly, slowly, creeping death are the malevolence goals
Genocide is still genocide in dribs and drabs
A million here and another million there
We have got to fucking care
The white horseman galloping around is so utterly bad
Scales of judgement held above and aloft
Waiting for angels to save us from our loss

But they are too sad and cross
We better pull through this death and destruction at any cost
The apocalypse takes no prisoners there is no question
That our current road is causing global indigestion
We need to grow and bury our differences
Evolve our attitude into some benevolent wisdoms
So, we can save our world from its own destructions
Save our world from the bombastic blundering us
There's no need to cuss just make a fuss
Fix one people, one place, or one thing with all our resources
Surely, we can fix just one place. One small country
Give it good grace
Save one people with schools and hospitals
Befriend another dwelling place and change its dire courses
To a future destination of a planet full of utopias
Not just another grim Hollywood dystopia
Will we ever see peace and prosperity in our lifetime?
Or are we seeing through eyes with permanent myopia
We are all living in a symbiotic clambering small world
How will our unknown futures twist and unfurl?

Writer's Revenge

It's true, you can write a book,
To get revenge for an injustice you took
Satisfy your painful heart's constant mood
Stand up to the bully is that understood
Whether fiction or fact it's the process that counts
Every word you write mounts and mounts
Imagine a telephone book being smacked in your mouth
Imagine the legs stumbling before they head south
There's no need to be vicious like a monster trapped in a cage
Just dish it out like you're on minimum wage
An internal knockout blow for the demons inside
Invisible creatures that won't let it slide
Write a book, satisfaction guaranteed
Muster the troops cause we're going to be freed
From revenges incessant justice fuelled desires
Plough your heart into the book burning pyres
Give no quarter and make it heartfelt
Because maybe one day you'll have something to sell
Karma could be kind and balance the books
And you could sit cosy in your inglenook

Yesterday

Yesterday I found my soul hiding
Trapped down a rocky crevasse
Crying help echoing up to find someone
Someone whose soul was gliding past
I am liberty, freedom, peace, and a very long kiss
Reaching, reaching for the realms of eternal bliss
But now you must climb up the crooked path
Work you ass off if you want to have a blast
of exotic mellowness
Reach the flower that stares down at your last
Handhold gripping an inch more of grass
On your ascension to peace and tranquillity
Escape the mundane. Tune in again to the energy
The synergy of feelings long lost to doldrums
Meaningful meditations away from all the knots and tantrums
Relax, put your feet up, sprawl across the rug
Skyward spiralling into a new dimension drug
Look at the ceiling, for at least a split second
And wonder where it goes in a brief assessment
Immerse yourself in an elixir from the heavens
A prescription pad for all occasions
Starlight distilled to a sparkle and feed
A vacantly shattered reflection of all deeds
New meds, new life, new seeds indeed
Flowers for the attic in times of need

You Bring The Light In
Swoosh, Swish, swirl, smile a smile of kindness
Your presence is an exercise in mindfulness
My heart dances for a while, while you approach
If you were a waterfall I'd choose to be soaked
Your voice, your touch is simply angelic music to my ears
Bringing warmth, love, and tenderness to all my fears
How does the world cope with these divine sensations
Locked in orbit around you with their own frustrations
Seeking solace from your loving compassionate soul
Rising high to greet you because they've always known
You are the light of life shining hope into our hearts
A quickening pulse is where everything starts
A connection to be made by our entranced spirit
And your heart holds on tight until you reach your limit

Acknowledgements

Thanks to Meek at Inherit The Earth, and to anyone else who contributes to my journey through this life.

Steven
July
2024

Also by Steven
Stabilizer
ISBN: 9798851038631

The Wrong Messiah
ISBN: 9798851040641

Nuts And Thunderbolts
ISBN: 9798854318761

EXOTIC SPECIES
ISBN: 9798852901507
Steven Joseph McCrystal
&
CT Meek

Monkey Spit
ISBN: 9798850961633

Red Pill Memories
ISBN: 9798850967970

Available from Amazon and major bookstores

Online publishing

inherit_theearth@btinternet.com

Notes

Amazon KDP

Printed in Great Britain
by Amazon